FRIENDS FROM AROUND THE WORLD

Early Learning Activities That Teach Global and Self-Awareness

by Patty Claycomb
illustrated by Marilynn G. Barr

This book is dedicated with love to:
❤ Rachael Claycomb ❤

Publisher: Roberta Suid
Copy Editor: Carol Whiteley
Senior Editor: Annalisa Suid
Production: Santa Monica Press
Educational Consultant: Sarah Felstiner

For a complete catalog of our products, please write to the address below:
P.O. Box 1680, Palo Alto, CA 94302

Monday Morning is a registered trademark of
Monday Morning Books, Inc.

ISBN: 1-878279-24-6

Printed in the United States of America

987654321

CONTENTS

INTRODUCTION

In order to understand people from other cultures, children must first discover more about themselves. Because once children like themselves, they will be ready to make friends with others. To this end, the activities, and patterns in *Friends from Around the World* promote self-awareness and self-esteem, as well as help children become aware of other cultures.

Friends are often people we grow up with—neighborhood buddies and schoolmates. But it's important to remind your students that while their best pal may live right next door, there is a world filled with people just waiting to be their friends. While children might have to travel thousands of miles to take part in a game of Yoté or to taste a bite of authentic Calcutta cuisine, it is possible to bring faraway sights, sounds, and foods right into the classroom.

By teaching your students skills for getting along and by exposing them to other cultures, you will encourage them to become friends with people nearby and from around the world. Engage your students in multicultural activities and they will develop so much: an *appreciation* of each other's similarities and differences; an *expanded world view* that includes respect for other countries and cultures; *skills* for living in a global society, such as communication, tolerance, and cooperation; and *concern* for all people.

Friends from Around the World is filled with art and movement activities, games, new songs set to familiar tunes, chants, bulletin board patterns, and more. Each chapter ends with a class project—a cooperative experience that links the lessons and activities in the unit.

Chapter One, "All About Me," helps children build self-esteem and self-awareness. Activities such as "Alike and Different" and "VIP Awards" let children explore their sense of self. The "Marvelous Me Class Project" ties the activities together. Children work cooperatively to create a classroom display that is all about *themselves*.

Chapter Two, "Me and My Friends," lets children establish friendships while building a sense of classroom community. "Best Friends" and "Friendship Fiesta" celebrate the concept of being friendly. The "Friendship Fun-Fest Class Project" lets children organize their work for this unit, display art, and play games.

Chapter Three, "Children from Many Lands," introduces children to foods, houses, and traditions from other countries. Children explore China, France, Israel, Mexico, India, and other locations. The "Our World Class Project" emphasizes the differences in these countries.

Chapter Four, "Fun and Games Around the World," is filled with active learning projects, songs, and creative games to increase children's global awareness. "Your Passport, Please" is the final classroom project, and allows children to imagine that they are world travelers.

By learning about themselves, their friends, and other cultures, children will gain the sense that they can make "friends from around the world."

CHAPTER ONE: ALL ABOUT ME

The projects, games, and activities in this unit encourage children to learn about themselves while building self-esteem. "Wonderful Me" lets children list the many reasons why they like themselves. "Feelings Concentration" is a game that helps children explore their feelings, emphasizing that it's okay to feel many different ways. "Family Ties" and "Families Forever" build on the bonds between children and their care-givers: parents, grandparents, guardians, baby sitters, and extended family members.

The Book Link with each activity will help you emphasize an assortment of important lessons, such as helping others (*To Hilda for Helping*), surviving sibling rivalry (*Julius, the Baby of the World*), sharing (*The Rainbow Fish*), and recognizing feelings (*Everybody Has Feelings*).

All the fun and interesting activities in this chapter will help each child in your class feel unique and special, while preparing him or her to learn more about children in other cultures.

©1995 Monday Morning Books, Inc.

ALIKE AND DIFFERENT

Teacher's Note:
Discuss the idea that people can be alike and different at the same time. Ask questions regarding likes and differences, such as, "Do you have ears?" (expect laughter). "Do you see someone else with ears?" "Are you wearing red socks?" "Do you see socks that are a different color than yours?"

Materials & Preparation:
None.

Directions:
1. Have the children sit in a circle on the rug, or outside on the lawn.
2. Ask for two children to volunteer to stand in the middle of the circle.
3. Have the rest of the children observe the two: their clothes, type of shoes, hair color, eye color, and so on.
4. Ask the children in the group to list the two children's similarities and differences.
5. Have the two partners decide whether they have more similarities or differences. Then have them sit down and choose two new children for the group to observe.
6. Continue play until every child has had a chance to be observed. If there is an odd number of children in your class, partner yourself with the last child.

Book Link:
• *We Are All Alike . . . We Are All Different* written and illustrated by the Cheltenham Elementary School Kindergartners, photos by Laura Dwight (Scholastic, 1991). Begin the activity by reading this book.

• *I'll Be You and You Be Me* by Ruth Krauss, illustrated by Maurice Sendak (The Bookstore Press, 1973). Read sections of this book to small groups.

BIRTHDAY BOOKS

Teacher's Note:
Ask the children if they remember when they were born. Have them brainstorm skills they have mastered since then. Stress the idea that all of them should be proud of their achievements.

Materials:
One birthday cake pattern page per child, a black felt pen, crayons, stickers, sticky stars, hole punch, yarn

Preparation:
None.

Directions:
1. Give each child a birthday cake pattern page. In the center of the cake pattern, have the children illustrate a skill they have mastered since they were born, for example, walking, tying their shoes, riding a trike, making their bed.
2. Provide crayons, stickers, and sticky stars for children to use to decorate the rest of the cake.
3. Use a hole punch and yarn to bind the completed drawings into a Class Birthday Book.
4. Put the finished Birthday Book on a low shelf or table where children can look at it on their own. The children can add to the book during the year as they learn new skills.

Option:
Cover a bulletin board with "new baby" wrapping paper. Have children bring in their baby pictures and post the pictures on a bulletin board labeled "The Way We Were." Parents can fill out index cards listing their child's height and weight at birth and place and date of birth to post with the baby pictures. Add current photos of the children and print their names below.

Book Link:
• *Benjamin's 365 Birthdays* by Judi Barrett, illustrated by Ron Barrett (Atheneum, 1974).
Benjamin celebrates his birthday every day of the year!
• *Happy Birthdays 'Round the World* by Lois S. Johnson, illustrated by Genia (Rand McNally, 1963).
This book explores the ways birthdays are celebrated in many different countries.

BIRTHDAY CAKE PATTERN

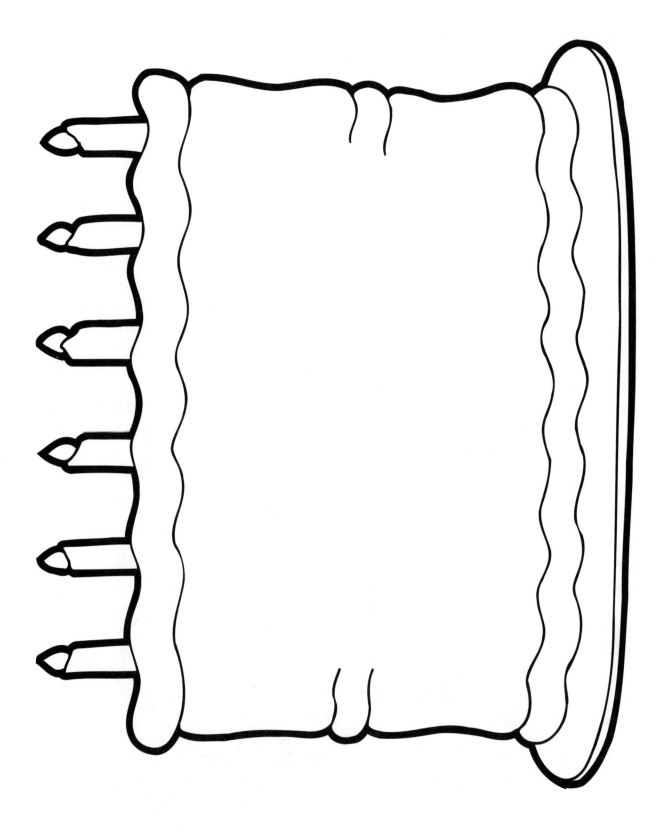

FAMILIES FOREVER

Teacher's Note:
Tell the children that lions roam in a pride, cows in a herd, and geese in a gaggle. Ask the question, "Do you live in a pride, a herd, or a family?" Have the children list the people in their immediate family.

Materials:
Family patterns, oak tag, crayons, people-colored paper, scissors, Popsicle sticks or straws, tape, craft knife

Preparation:
Duplicate the family patterns onto oak tag and cut out with a craft knife to make templates. Use both the "positives" and "negatives" for children to trace in and around.

Directions:
1. Children can trace the oak tag templates that fit their family configuration, for example, one girl, one mother, and one father. Provide paper in people colors for children to choose from.
2. Have the children draw faces onto their patterns, including their own, and cut them out. (You can also provide pre-cut patterns for those children who need help.)
3. Provide straws or Popsicle sticks for children to tape to the back of their family cutouts to make puppets.
4. Children can use these family puppets to recreate scenes from their own families. Invite children to introduce their family member puppets to the rest of the class.

Note:
Save the "Families Forever" cutouts for use in "Home Sweet Home" (p. 18).

Option:
Have children bring in family pictures to post on a "Family Portraits" bulletin board or in a Family Photo Album.

Book Link:
• *A Cache of Jewels and Other Collective Nouns* by Ruth Heller (Grosset & Dunlap, 1987).
Brief text and brilliantly colored illustrations explain the names for groups of items, such as a batch of bread and a school of fish.

FAMILY PATTERNS

FAMILY TIES

Teacher's Note:
Discuss the people who make up a family beyond immediate family members: grandmothers, grandfathers, aunts, uncles, cousins, great-aunts, and great-uncles. Ask the children if they are happy to be related to so many people.

Materials:
Extended family pattern, paper in people colors, crayons or markers, scissors, colored construction paper, glue

Preparation:
Duplicate the extended family pattern onto people-colored paper for children to choose from.

Directions:
1. Have the children color their extended family members pattern.
2. Children can cut apart their patterns or leave them all together. Note: If some parts of the pattern don't relate to their own families, children can cut out the pieces that fit and glue them to another color of construction paper backing.
3. Have the children sit together. Encourage them in turn to hold up their drawing and share something special about their family.

Book Link:
• *Catspring, Somersault, Flying One-Handed Flip-Flop* by Suann Kiser, illustrated by Peter Catalanotto (Orchard, 1993).
It's hard to feel special in a crowded family of 12, but Katie manages just fine!

• *Uproar on Hollercat Hill* by Jean Marzollo, illustrated by Steven Kellogg (Dial, 1980).
Even though tempers flare in this busy family, love conquers all.

EXTENDED FAMILY PATTERN

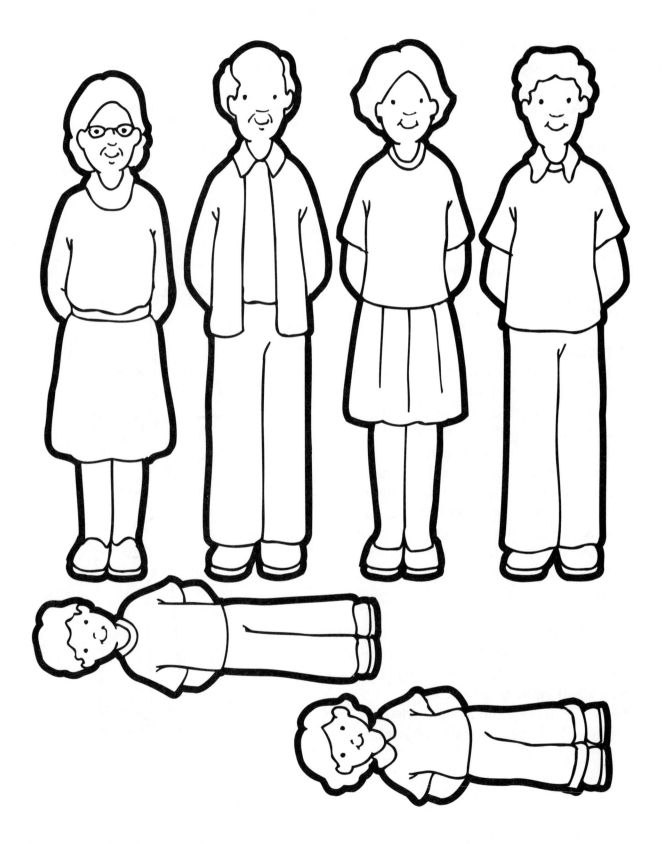

FEELINGS CONCENTRATION

Teacher's Note:
Talk about the many different kinds of feelings that are possible. People can feel happy, sad, mad, scared, lonely, proud, hurt, sleepy, and more. Ask each child how he or she feels, and encourage the idea that all feelings are okay, and that people should like themselves no matter how they are feeling.

Materials:
Concentration game pieces pattern, markers, scissors

Preparation:
Duplicate the game pieces (make two copies of each), color, laminate, and cut out.

Directions:
1. Place the 24 cards face up on the rug or a table.
2. Point out the twelve different feelings that are represented and their matching pairs.
3. Mix up the cards and turn them face down on the rug.
4. Have the children pair up to play the game as they would play "Concentration." One child turns over two cards. If the cards match, the child keeps the two cards and tries again. If a match is not made, the cards are replaced and the other child takes a turn.
5. As each card is turned over, have both children name the feeling that is revealed.
6. Play continues until all cards are matched.

Option:
Have the children imitate the feelings faces. They can list reasons for what makes them feel different ways.

Book Link:
• *Everybody Has Feelings: Todos Tenemos Sentimientos* text and photos by Charles E. Avery (Open Hand, 1992).
This book has beautiful black and white photos of all kinds of feelings, even mixed-up ones. The text is bilingual, English and Spanish.
• *Feelings* by Aliki (Greenwillow, 1984). "How do you feel? Angry? Sad? Read this book and you'll feel terrific!"

CONCENTRATION GAME PIECES

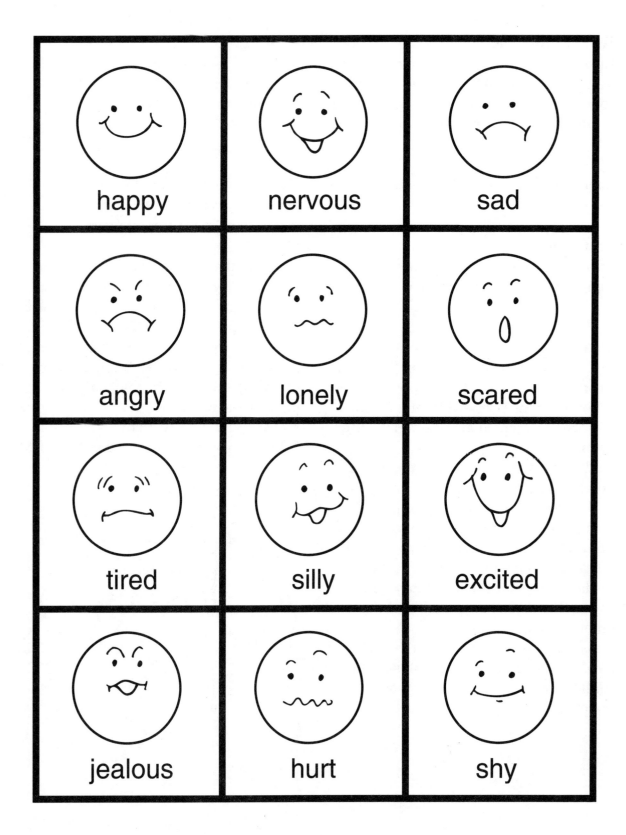

GLITTER LETTERS

Teacher's Note:
Write the ABCs on the chalkboard. Point out to the children that the alphabet is a set of letters, the letters stand for sounds, and the sounds make up words. Have everyone sing the ABC song together.

Materials:
Paper, a pencil, markers, crayons, glue in small squeeze bottles (or glue in cups with paintbrushes), glitter

Preparation:
Print each child's name on a separate sheet of paper. Make the letters at least two inches high.

Directions:
1. Provide markers and crayons for children to use to decorate their names.
2. Show children how to trace the letters with glue and then sprinkle glitter over the glue for a sparkly effect.
3. Display the names on a bulletin board. Have the children observe how beautiful their names look!

Book Link:
• *Chrysanthemum* by Kevin Henkes (Greenwillow, 1991).
Chrysanthemum loves her name, until she begins school and the other mice tease her. Luckily, a wonderful teacher named Delphinium Twinkle renews Chrysanthemum's self-confidence.

HEART ART

Teacher's Note:
Ask the children to list the different people and animals they love. Possible answers might be: parents, brothers, sisters, babies, grandparents, friends, teachers, and pets. Remind the children that they should add themselves to their lists.

Materials:
One heart pattern per child, crayons, watercolors, paintbrushes

Preparation:
None.

Directions:
1. Ask the children to brainstorm at least three things that they love about themselves. For example, "I love my smile, my freckles, and the way I ride my trike."
2. Give each child a pattern and explain that the three hearts represent three things that children love about themselves.
3. Provide crayons, watercolors, and paintbrushes for children to use to make watercolor resist paintings.
4. Post the hearts on a bulletin board and have the children look at their "heart-y art."

Option:
Cover the bulletin board in heart-patterned wrapping paper before posting the heart-shaped pictures. (Heart-patterned paper is usually available at stationery stores around Valentine's Day.) Or use red and pink construction paper for the background.

Book Link:
• *I Like Me!* by Nancy Carlson (Viking, 1988).
The pretty pig in this story lists all the reasons that she likes herself.
• *Valentine's Day* by Fern G. Brown (Franklin Watts, 1983).
This resource is filled with interesting Valentine's Day info.

HEART PATTERN

HOME SWEET HOME

Teacher's Note:
Discuss the different types of dwellings that people choose to live in, including houses, apartments, trailers, houseboats, tents, castles, tepees, and igloos.

Materials:
Assorted boxes (shoe boxes, cereal boxes, milk cartons), construction paper, scissors, crayons or markers, glue, tape, cellophane, wrapping paper and wallpaper scraps, family patterns (p. 10)

Preparation:
None.

Directions:
1. Children can use a variety of the materials listed above to make replicas of their houses. Empty boxes work for the base, and construction paper, wallpaper scraps, and cellophane can be used to decorate the inside and outside.
2. When the houses are finished, children can tape or glue their family members to the front of the houses or set them inside.
3. Have the children sit together on the rug and share their unique houses.
4. Set up a "Home Sweet Home" display on a table or shelf.

Book Link:
• *How We Live* by Anita Harper, illustrated by Christine Roche (Harper, 1977). This book covers a variety of dwellings and family configurations.

• *A House Is a House for Me* by Mary Ann Hoberman, illustrated by Betty Fraser. "A web is a house for a spider . . . and a house is a house for me!"

THE "IN" CROWD

Teacher's Note:
Have the children stand close together. Discuss the fact that in a crowd, it is easy to feel ignored or left out. Remind the students that no matter how many people are in a group, nobody should feel less important than anyone else.

Materials:
Paper plates (one per child), crayons, hand mirrors, scissors, tape

Preparation:
None.

Directions:
1. Have the children use the hand mirrors to observe their hair style, hair color, eye color, freckles, and so on.
2. Give each child a paper plate to decorate to look like his or her own face.
3. Tape the plates close together on a wall.
4. Have the children sit on the floor and observe the crowd of paper faces.
5. Ask each child, in turn, to find him- or herself in the crowd.
6. Ask the children questions, such as, "How did you find yourself?" "Is there someone else in the crowd who looks like you?" "Should you feel important even when you're in a large crowd?" (Yes!)

Book Link:
• *Mushroom in the Rain* by Mirra Ginsburg, illustrated by Jose Aruego and Ariane Dewey (Macmillan, 1974). During a rainstorm, an ever-growing crowd of animals huddles under a mushroom cap. How do all those animals fit under a little mushroom?

RAINBOW SKIN

Teacher's Note:
Have the children point out the areas of their bodies where they see skin. Encourage the students to compare their skin tones, focusing on the idea that all people's skin looks good on them!

Materials:
Scissors, butcher paper, crayons, tape

Preparation:
Cut a two-foot-long strip of butcher paper for each child.

Directions:
1. Help each child trace one arm (from shoulder to fingertips) onto his or her paper.
2. Children can use crayons to color their pictures any shade they wish.
3. When the pictures are finished, have the children cut around the traced outlines.
4. Tape the cutouts in a large circle with the hands pointing inward to form a communal design.
5. Have the children sit on the rug and observe the pattern of hands and arms.
6. Ask the children what the pictures remind them of. Possible responses are "helping each other," "being friends," and "holding hands."

Option:
On a large sheet of butcher paper, trace a life-size outline of a person. Have the children color the figure with crayons. Post the picture on a wall, and label it "People Come in Beautiful Colors!"

Book Link:
• *A Color of His Own* by Leo Lionni (Pantheon, 1975).
A lonely chameleon learns to enjoy his ever-changing skin color.
• *The Land of Many Colors* by the Klamath County YMCA Family Preschool (Scholastic, 1993).
Blue, green, and purple people learn to get together and make their world a happier place.

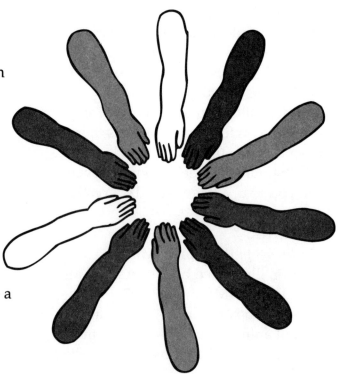

SCHOOL OF FISH

Teacher's Note:
Tell the children that a group of fish swimming together is called a "school." Have the children swim around slowly and pretend to be a school of swimming people fish. Remind the students that even though they are all in a group, each person is a unique and special individual.

Materials:
One fish pattern per child, crayons, scissors, yarn, hole punch

Preparation:
None.

Directions:
1. Have the children color their fish patterns. They can decorate their fish with rainbows, stripes, circles, and other shapes.
2. When the pictures are finished, have the children cut out their fish.
3. Help the children punch a hole in the top edge of their fish patterns.
4. Thread a length of yarn through each fish and secure with a knot.
5. Have children form a "school" on the rug, each child holding his or her fish by the string and making it "swim" by moving the string.
6. Choose one child to be the leader and lead the children and their fish around the classroom. Give every child the turn to be leader.

Option:
Provide swimming accessories for children to wear while they walk with their fish. These could include flippers, goggles, masks, bathing caps, and so on.

Book Link:
• *Swimmy* by Leo Lionni (Pantheon, 1968). When a school of little fish swims together, they scare away the hungry sharks.
• *The Rainbow Fish* by Marcus Pfister (North-South, 1992). A beautiful fish with silver scales learns how to share and make friends.

FISH PATTERN

THE THREE BEARS FAMILY

Teacher's Note:
Present the idea that everyone plays an important part in his or her family. Ask the children to think of the jobs that their parents and siblings perform for the family; include babies and pets. Then ask the children, in turn, to say what their own favorite job is in their family.

Materials:
Three Bears patterns, Contact paper, flannel board, felt or tape, scissors, crayons

Preparation:
Duplicate the flannel board patterns, color, cover with Contact paper for added sturdiness, and cut out. Back with a small piece of felt or a tape loop so the pieces stick to the flannel board.

Directions:
1. Tell the story of "The Three Bears" using the flannel board patterns.
2. As you tell the story, point out the family roles of the papa, mama, and baby.
3. After you tell the story, ask the children to list the roles each bear played. Ask who the children would like to be in the story.
4. Have the children brainstorm the types of roles people play in their families. Refer to *Hooray for Me!* (p. 27) to reinforce the concept that people can play many roles at the same time!

Option:
Duplicate the patterns for each child to retell the story on his or her own. Children may color in the patterns and use them as puppets.

Book Link:
• *Julius, the Baby of the World* by Kevin Henkes (Greenwillow, 1990).
Lilly is unimpressed with the importance of Julius' role in the family, but a confrontation with a cousin helps change Lilly's opinion.

THE THREE BEARS PATTERNS

VIP AWARDS

Teacher's Note:
VIP = Very Important Person! Have the children think of reasons why they feel important. If any children need help with ideas, point out various positive traits: super smiler, marvelous musician, amazing artist, fabulous friend. . . .

Materials:
One small paper plate per child, star stickers, glitter, glue, crayons, scissors, ribbons, yarn, pen, tape

Preparation:
Print the letters "VIP" in the middle of each paper plate.

Directions:
1. Have the children use glitter, crayons, ribbons, and other materials to turn their paper plates into VIP awards.
2. When the awards are finished, help the children write their names on the plates.
3. Collect the awards and have the class sit in a circle on the rug.
4. Read the name of each child and have that child come forward to receive his or her award. Use loops of tape to attach the awards to the children's clothes. Be sure to tell the children how important they are as they accept their awards.

Option:
Make a giant classroom award. Print the letters "VIP" in the center of a large butcher-paper circle three feet in diameter. Have the children work together to decorate the award using ribbons, glitter, stickers, and so on.

Book Link:
• *To Hilda for Helping* by Margot Zemach (Farrar, 1977).
Hilda receives a home-made VIP award for being such a good helper.

WHAT'S YOUR NAME?

Teacher's Note:
Explain that people in different countries speak different languages. Play tapes from a variety of languages. Choose language lesson tapes, or recordings of singing in other languages. If any of the children speak other languages, have them or their parents speak to the class.

Materials & Preparation:
None.

Directions:
1. Have the children stand one by one and say, "Hello, my name is _____."
2. Have everyone repeat the sentence above in Spanish. "Hola, me llamo _____" (O-la, may ya-mo _____).
3. Continue repeating sentences using different languages. (In Arabic it is, "Mar-huba, iss-mee _____.")

Option:
Sing "The Good Morning Song" in English, and then in German ("Guten Morgen"), in Dutch ("Goede Morgen"), in Swedish ("God Morgen"), in French ("Bon Jour"), in Italian ("Buon Giorno"), and in Hebrew ("Boker Tov").

The Good Morning Song
(to the tune of "Happy Birthday")
Good morning to you,
Good morning to you,
Good morning, dear children,
Good morning to you.

WONDERFUL ME

Teacher's Note:
Before beginning this activity, have children think of reasons why they like their friends. Set aside a certain amount of time for children to tell their friends why they like them. Then have the students brainstorm reasons why they like themselves.

Materials:
Butcher paper, felt markers, scissors, tape, sticky stars

Preparation:
Trace the outline of a child onto butcher paper, cut it out, and tape it on a wall. Print "I like myself because . . ." in the middle of the paper body. (You need to cut out only one figure for the entire class.)

Directions:
1. Have the children sit on the rug, next to the paper figure.
2. Explain that they will each, in turn, finish the sentence.
3. As a child responds, print his or her answer with a marker inside the outline of the figure. Print each child's name by his or her answer.
4. Let the child place sticky stars by his or her response.
5. Have the children observe the completed figure. Point out the many reasons there are for people to like themselves.

Book Link:
• *Hooray for Me!* by Remy Charlip and Lilian Moore, paintings by Vera B. Williams (Parents' Magazine Press, 1975). Characters in this book relate their various identities: "I am my mother and father's daughter," "I am my cat's pillow," "I am my dog's walker," "I am my body's shadow."

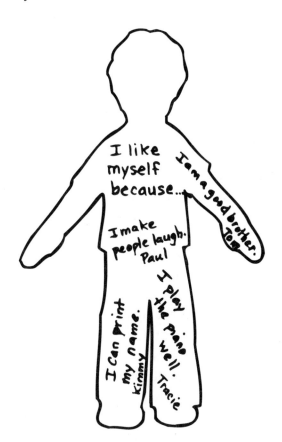

MARVELOUS ME CLASS PROJECT

Teacher's Note:
This final project incorporates the results of many of the activities from the "All About Me" chapter. Allow children to do as much of the work as possible in creating this "Me Mural." Invite parents, friends, and other classes to admire it. Provide a Classroom Sign-in notebook for guests to give their impressions of the artwork.

Materials:
Completed artwork projects from this unit, posting tools (tape, yarn, etc.), paper, notebook, pen

Preparation:
Clear a wall, bulletin board, several windows, or a table that the children choose for the display area.

Directions:
1. Help the children organize their work from this unit, and provide the necessary tools for posting some of their different completed projects. The hands and arms touching from "Rainbow Skin" could be a border on a table that holds some "Birthday Books." "Glitter Letter" names could run along the top of the bulletin board. The "Families Forever," "Home Sweet Home," and "Family Ties" art could make up a central bulletin board and table display. "VIP Awards" make a great hallway display. A crowd of paper plate faces from "The 'In' Crowd" could look on from across the room. Make sure that at least one piece of each child's is displayed.
2. Children can compose a brief description of their artwork display, each listing feelings about the completed work. Copy

their statements onto a program and duplicate for classroom guests.

Option:
Play background music, such as "Free to Be You and Me" (Marlo Thomas), "The Rainbow Connection" (Kermit the Frog), or "One Was Johnny" (Carole King), while children work cooperatively.

CHAPTER TWO: ME AND MY FRIENDS

The activities in this chapter promote cooperation and teamwork. Children will brainstorm their own answers to questions such as, "What makes a best friend?" (in "Best Friends") and "Who can I be friends with?" ("Rainbow Friends").

Your students will begin to understand and appreciate their friendships, while feeling as if they are each an important part of the larger group.

Book Links will help you emphasize a variety of lessons, such as the concept that friends don't always agree (*What I Like*), the fact that friends can come from different backgrounds (*Yo! Yes?*), and the idea that friends like many qualities about each other, even silly things (*Rosie and Michael*)!

These fun and interesting activities will help the children in your class build new friendships and strengthen existing ones.

BEST FRIENDS

Teacher's Note:
Ask the question, "What is a best friend?" Possible answers include, "Someone who you play with the most," or "Someone who makes you feel special." Discuss the idea that a best friend can be a friend for many years.

Materials:
Friend patterns, scissors, felt pens, crayons

Preparation:
Duplicate and cut out the best friend cards. (Laminate if desired.)

Directions:
1. Give the children a chance to look at the cards before placing the cards face down on a rug or table.
2. Each child, in turn, can turn over two cards. If the cards match, the child keeps the pair and takes another turn. If the cards don't match, another child takes a turn.
3. Let the children use crayons to color the matches they keep.
4. Keep the finished "Friend Cards" to play with again on another day.

Option:
Fold a paper in half and draw a human outline. The end of one arm and leg should be touching the folded edge. Cut this figure out. There should be two best friends connected by their arms! Make enough cutouts so that each child can have one to color—one shape like him- or herself and the remaining figure like his or her best friend.

Book Link:
• *Rosie and Michael* by Judith Viorst, illustrated by Lorna Tomei (Atheneum, 1975).
Rosie and Michael are best friends, even though they occasionally tease or play a few tricks on each other.
• *Best Friends for Frances* by Russell Hoban (Harper, 1969).
When Albert and his pals have a "no girls" basketball game, Frances and Gloria go on their own special outing: "No boys."

FRIEND PATTERNS

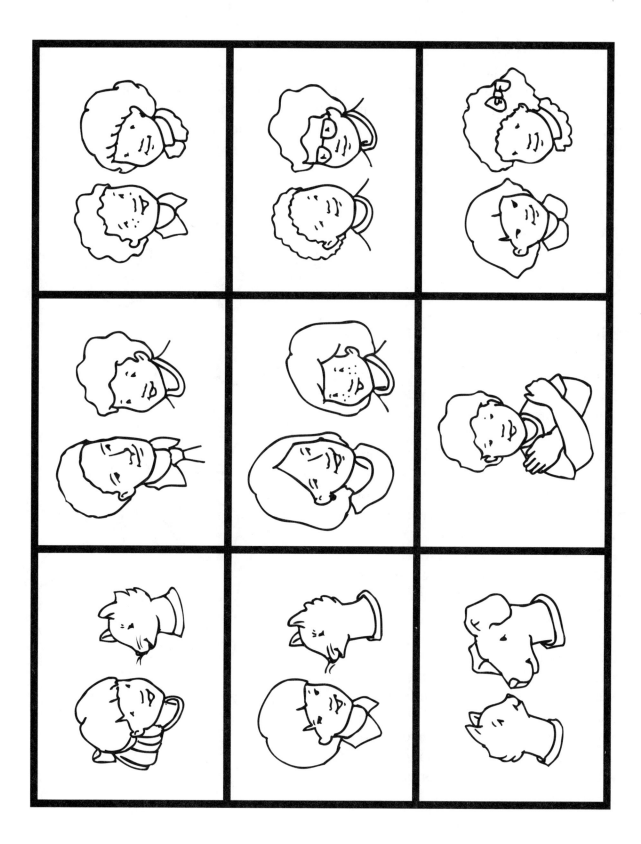

THE FRIENDSHIP DANCE

Teacher's Note:
Discuss the idea that friendship means *always*. You cannot "sometimes" be a friend. Ask the question, "If you are playing with a new friend, and an old friend wants to join you, what should you say?" Also reinforce the fact that it's okay to want time alone; it doesn't mean children are not still friends. Discuss the fact that people can have many friends, and that each friend should be treated with care.

Materials:
Recorded music

Preparation:
None.

Directions:
1. Start by having two friends dance together to the music.
2. Choose a time to stop the music. When this happens, have the children who are dancing each pick another friend to dance with. (Now there are two pairs dancing.)
3. Continue playing and stopping the music. At each break, the children should pick new partners until everyone is dancing "The Friendship Dance."
4. When all the children have danced, have them sit together on the rug. Reinforce the idea that no one was forgotten—everyone was asked to play!

Book Link:
• *The Perfect Pal* by Jack Gantos and Nicole Rubel (Houghton Mifflin, 1979). Vanessa looks for a pal at the pet store, but the pig makes a pig of herself, and the sloth sleeps through every dance. Luckily, Vanessa finds a surprise "perfect pal" at the end of the tale.

FRIENDSHIP FIESTA

Teacher's Note:
Ask the children to brainstorm reasons to celebrate, such as a birthday, a holiday
. . . or a friendship! Discuss the fact that friendships are worth celebrating and
ask children to plan a Friendship Fiesta.

Materials:
Balloon pattern, crayons, markers, glitter, glue, recorded music, party hats, noise-makers, streamers

Preparation:
Duplicate the balloon pattern for each child.

Directions:
1. Have the children decorate the balloon patterns using crayons, markers, glitter, and glue.
2. When the pictures are done, the children can help decorate the room with their balloons and with streamers.
3. Pass out party hats and noisemakers. Put on festive music, such as tapes by The Beach Boys, and let the children dance.
4. Read party books and friendship books. Keep these in the Book Nook for children to look through later.

Option:
Take photos of your Friendship Fiesta, and post them on a bulletin board to remind children of the fun they had!

Book Link:
• *Fiesta* by June Behrens, photographs by Scott Taylor (Children's Press, 1978). Short text and color photos make this book a perfect read-aloud.

• *Fiesta! Mexico's Great Celebrations* by Elizabeth Silverthorne (Millbrook, 1992). This resource includes recipes, craft ideas, and a glossary.

BALLOON PATTERN

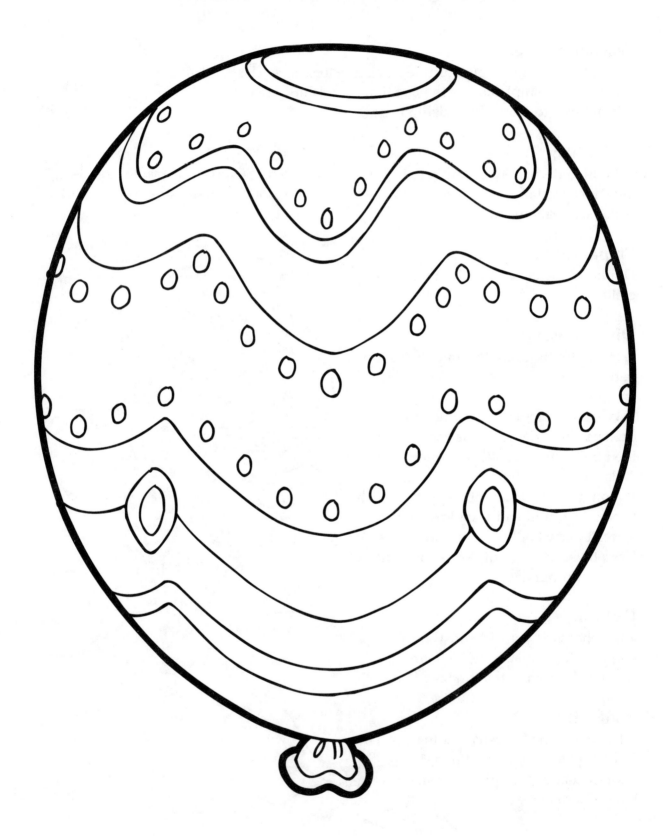

FRIENDSHIP GIFTS

Teacher's Note:
Describe the concept of friendship as something as special as a wonderful gift. Ask the children if they are excited when they receive a gift. It is the same feeling with friendship. If people give their friendship, they have given something very special. Friendship should be treated with care and respect!

Materials:
Gift box pattern, markers, crayons, stickers, glitter, glue, ribbon, tape

Preparation:
Duplicate the gift box pattern for each child.

Directions:
1. Have the children draw beautiful designs on their gift box with crayons and markers.
2. Provide stickers, glitter, and ribbons for children to use to decorate their "gift."
3. When the children have finished decorating their gift box, invite them to sit together on the rug.
4. Sing a chorus of "Love Is Like a Magic Penny" or "Glad to Have a Friend Like You" (from *Free to Be You and Me*), and remind children to think of friendship as a gift to be given away. The children can exchange their friendship "gift boxes" or they can give them to someone in their family.

Book Link:
• *Mr. Rabbit's Lovely Present* by Charlotte Zolotow, illustrated by Maurice Sendak (Harper, 1962).
Mr. Rabbit helps his friend put together a perfect gift for her mother.

• *Frog and Toad Are Friends* by Arnold Lobel (Harper, 1970).
This "I Can Read" book recounts the adventures of two best friends. It is also available as a video-recording (Churchill Films, 1985).

GIFT BOX PATTERN

FRIENDSHIP TOWN

Teacher's Note:

Discuss the concept of living in a neighborhood or town where everyone knows and likes each other. Have children decide whether their town is a friendly town. They might think of places they know that are friendly, such as Mr. Roger's neighborhood or their own neighborhood!

Materials:

Friendship people patterns, friendship town patterns, crayons, tempera paint, paintbrushes, markers, empty boxes and containers, glue, construction paper, scissors, blocks (optional)

Preparation:

Duplicate the friendship patterns for each child.

Directions:

1. Give each child a copy of the friendship people patterns to color and cut out.
2. Give each child a copy of the friendship town patterns to color and cut out.
3. Provide empty boxes, cardboard tubes, milk cartons, and other containers for children to decorate with tempera paints, markers, and crayons. Or children can build a Friendship Town out of blocks.
4. Let children use the patterns and boxes to create a Friendship Town. They can set up the town on a table or on the floor. Friendship people patterns can be folded over at the base to help them stand up. Children can act out various daily duties in their town.
5. Enlarge the Friendship Town sign and post it near the town.

Option:

Place plastic cars, trucks, and animals near the Friendship Town for children to incorporate into their play. Other manipulatives, such as dolls, furniture, etc., may also be added.

Book Link:

• *The Friends of Emily Culpepper* by Ann Coleridge, illustrated by Roland Harvey (Putnam's, 1983).
When Emily's friends come to visit, they have a difficult time going home.

FRIENDSHIP PEOPLE PATTERNS

FRIENDSHIP TOWN PATTERNS

STOP

MAIL

Book Store

BAKERY

Friendship Town

GIVE AND TAKE

Teacher's Note:
Talk about the idea of give and take in a friendship. Ask children to share a time when they have made a friend happy. Ask the question, "Can you remember when someone made you happy?" Encourage the idea that making someone else happy means that you care about someone, besides yourself.

Materials & Preparation:
None.

Directions:
1. Have the children choose partners.
2. Ask the partners to sit facing each other.
3. Have the partners hold hands at shoulder level so each child can easily apply gentle force.
4. Have the children practice rocking in a back-and-forth motion.
5. While the children are rocking, teach them to sing "The Give and Take Song" (to the tune of "Row, Row, Row Your Boat").
6. The children can rock back and forth in different ways: very slowly, fast, in a circular motion, and side to side.
7. Reinforce the idea that it takes both friends to make a friendship work!

The Give and Take Song
Give, give, give, and take,
When you have a friend.
Happily, happily, happily, happily,
Stay friends to the end!

Book Link:
• *What I Like* by Catherine and Lawrence Anholt (Putnam's, 1991).
This is a fun story told in rhyme about friends who like and dislike different things. What happens when friends disagree? Find out! The simple, colorful illustrations are delightful.

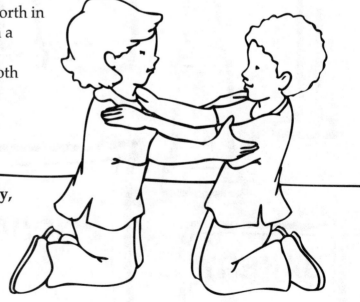

POCKET PALS

Teacher's Note:
Tell the children that they are going to make a friend that they can carry around with them—a Pocket Pal! When they're done making this Popsicle friend, they might make a second for a real live friend.

Materials:
Popsicle sticks, glue, colored yarn, scissors, markers, felt scraps

Preparation:
None.

Directions:
1. The children can use the markers to draw faces on the Popsicle sticks. Yarn can be glued on the sticks for hair, and felt scrap clothes can also be glued on. Encourage the children to make as many friends as they want.
2. When the children are finished, help them print their name on the backs of their Popsicle-stick friends.
3. Have the children gather up their Pocket Pals and sit together on the rug. They can place their Popsicle sticks in front of them.
4. Each child, in turn, can introduce his or her new friend. Ask questions such as, "What is your Pocket Pal's favorite color?" "What games could you play with your Pocket Pal?"

Option:
Let the children put on puppet shows with their Pocket Pals. Two children at a time may kneel behind a desk "stage."

Book Link:
• *Making Friends* by Fred Rogers, photographs by Jim Judkis (Putnam's, 1987). Mr. Rogers knows a lot about kids, and a lot about friends!

RAINBOW FRIENDS

Teacher's Note:
Have the children look around the class at the other students. Have each child describe a friend; remind children that friends do not have to look alike. Ask questions, such as, "Could a grownup be friends with a child?" "Could a boy be friends with a girl?" "Could a dog be friends with a child?"

Materials:
Body pattern, crayons and markers in people colors, scissors, tape

Preparation:
Duplicate a body pattern for each child.

Directions:
1. Have each child color in a body pattern to look like a friend.
2. Remind the children that a friend can be any color! Encourage them to add facial features, hair color, clothes, and so on. Ask everyone to color the entire face and body.
3. Have children cut out their completed pictures.
4. Tape the "friends" in a row—low on a wall. Tape them so the hands of the patterns are touching.

Option:
Trace the children's outlines on a large sheet of butcher paper. Have the children color their life-sized friend. When the pictures are finished, ask each child to tell you his or her friend's name. Print this name on the paper friend. Tape the drawings on a wall with hands touching.

Book Link:
• *Yo! Yes?* by Chris Raschka (Orchard, 1993).
Two young boys meet and become quick friends.
• *Earl's Too Cool for Me* by Leah Komaiko, illustrated by Laura Cornell (Harper, 1988).
Earl's pretty cool, but he's not too cool to be a friend.

BODY PATTERN

SAND DOLLAR STAR SEARCH

Teacher's Note:
Discuss the differences between playing in large and small groups. In a small group, it's easier to play and talk with each friend individually. Larger groups can become noisy, making it very important to share and cooperate. A strong team spirit will help group play go smoothly and, as a result, be more fun.

Materials:
Sand dollar pattern, pictures of sand dollars or actual sand dollars, scissors, marker, silver glitter, glue

Preparation:
Duplicate a sand dollar pattern for each child. Hide the patterns around the classroom.

Book Link:
• *The Sneetches and Other Stories* by Dr. Seuss (Random House, 1961).
The Sneetches with stars on their bellies think they are cooler than the ones without stars. But when the ones *without* get their own, and the ones *with* have them removed, it all gets too confusing for everyone!

Directions:
1. Show pictures of real sand dollars or, if possible, bring in a few for children to observe. Point out that a sand dollar has a shape like a star in its middle.
2. Have the children search for their sand dollar stars. Encourage a group effort!
3. When a child finds a sand dollar, that child can help friends who are still looking.
4. When all the sand dollars have been found, have the children sit together on the rug. Ask questions, such as, "Was it fun to work with a large group of friends?" "Did you help someone?" "Did you feel team spirit while you searched for your sand dollars?"
5. The children can further decorate their sand dollar pictures with silver glitter and glue. Post the completed sand dollars on a "Team Spirit" bulletin board.

SAND DOLLAR PATTERN

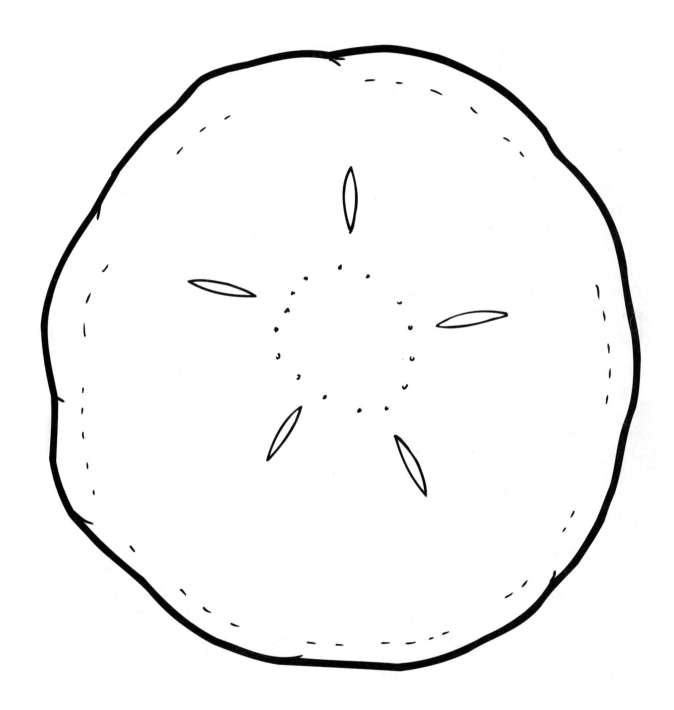

TEAM MACHINE

Teacher's Note:
Tell the children that a team is a group of people working together. Ask children to list any teams they know, such as their favorite sports teams or singing groups. Have the children sit in a circle on the floor and join hands. Create a team cheer together, for example, "We are a team! We work together!"

Materials:
3' x 4' sheet of butcher paper, scissors, tape, crayons or markers, package of stickers (enough for each child to have 1 or 2)

Preparation:
Tape a package of stickers to the wall. Tape the butcher paper sheet to the wall, covering the stickers. (The paper should be low enough for children to draw on it.)

Directions:
1. Explain that the children will form a team to create a large sticker-making machine. Reinforce the idea that the children should work together, and that each child will draw a part of the machine. All the parts of the machine must be connected.
2. When everyone has drawn part of the machine, have the children observe the finished product. Make sure that every child has participated in the creation.
3. Have the children join hands again and repeat their team chant. Ask them if they think the machine works. Then reveal the surprise stickers hidden behind the paper. Team work works! Hand out a sticker to each child to keep.

Option:
Children can use their bodies to form a moving machine. Each child acts out a type of movement (standing up and squatting down, turning in a circle), but must be touching another child at the same time. Children could pass the stickers along, from one to another, while they move in sequence.

WHAT MAKES A FRIEND?

Teacher's Note:
Encourage the idea that anyone, no matter how old, can be a friend. This includes a grandfather, a mother, and even a baby. Friends are people who like and care about each other.

Materials & Preparation:
None.

Directions:
1. Have the children learn "The Friendship Song." Sing it to the tune of "If You're Happy and You Know It."
2. Show the children how to act out movements to describe the friend. For example, for the word "listen," cup a hand over your ear. For the word "helps," put a hand forward, as if offering assistance. For the word "love," put your hand over your heart. Clap twice after "hands."

The Friendship Song
If you have a friend who listens, clap your hands.
If you have a friend who listens, clap your hands.
I would like to be your friend, to the very, very end.
If you have a friend who listens, clap your hands!

If you have a friend who helps you, clap your hands.
If you have a friend who helps you, clap your hands.
I would like to be your friend, to the very, very end.
If you have a friend who helps you, clap your hands!

If you have a friend who loves you, clap your hands.
If you have a friend who loves you, clap your hands.
I would like to be your friend, to the very, very end.
If you have a friend who loves you, clap your hands!

Book Link:
• *Friends* by Satomi Ichikawa (Parents' Magazine Press, 1976).
This book lists many reasons for needing friends, including, "We need friends for blowing bubbles at." Have children blow bubbles together after reading this book!
• *May I Bring a Friend* by Beatrice Schenk de Regniers, illustrated by Beni Montresor (Atheneum, 1964).
The narrator is invited to tea by the queen, and asks if he may bring a friend . . . from the zoo!

FRIENDSHIP FUN-FEST CLASS PROJECT

Teacher's Note:
This final project uses the results of many of the activities from the "Me and My Friends" chapter. Allow children to do as much of the work as possible in creating this friendship display. Invite parents, friends, and other classes to admire the completed work. Provide a Classroom Sign-in notebook for guests to give their impressions of the artwork.

Materials:
Completed artwork projects from this unit, posting tools (tape, notebook, yarn, etc.), paper, pen

Preparation:
Clear a wall, bulletin board, several windows, or a table that the children choose for the display area.

Directions:
1. Help the children organize their work from this unit, and provide the necessary tools for posting some of their completed projects. They can set up their "Friendship Town" on a low table with the Friendship Street signs on a bulletin board above it. "Pocket Pals" might be set in clear plastic cups as if watching the festivities. "Rainbow Friends" can be posted on a wall or bulletin board. The "Team Machine" will make a perfect wall hanging or, if done three-dimensionally, an impressive sculpture piece.
2. Children can invite guests to play a game of "Best Friends" concentration, or to sing "The Friendship Song" (p. 47).

3. Children can compose a brief description of their artwork display, each listing feelings about the completed work. Copy their statements onto a program and duplicate for classroom guests.

Option:
Play background music, such as "You've Got a Friend" (James Taylor), "That's What Friends Are For" (Dionne Warwick et al.), "Whenever I Call You Friend" (Kenny Loggins), or "My Friend" (Take 6) while children work cooperatively.

CHAPTER THREE: CHILDREN FROM MANY LANDS

This chapter gives children some small samples of life from other countries or continents. Your students will explore the amazing Amazon ("Life in the Rain Forest"), learn about unusual animals in "Animals in Australia," discover a bit of the lives of Chinese youngsters in "Children in China," create their own French perfume, and savor a taste (literally!) of snacks from Mexico and India. Finally, children will have the opportunity to work together to create a mini-world in their own classroom.

Patterns for these activities include cutouts of children from many of the different cultures. These patterns will be used in the "Our World Class Project" at the end of the chapter. However, you can also enlarge these patterns and post them on a multicultural bulletin board to introduce the "Children from Many Lands" unit.

The activities in this unit will help children learn to respect different cultures and ways of going about daily life in other countries, where customs may be drastically different from the way the children live at home.

Note: Provide globes, atlases, and maps for children to study (or just see on the walls) during the course of this unit. Children might also enjoy paging through magazines such as *National Geographic*, *Ranger Rick*, or travel magazines.

ANIMALS IN AUSTRALIA

Teacher's Note:
Tell the children that Australia is known for its interesting animals. Children may be able to name some of the animals, but you can help by listing koala bears, platypuses, kangaroos, and wallabies.

Materials:
Australian animal patterns, large sheets of drawing paper, small envelopes, tape or glue, crayons, scissors

Preparation:
Duplicate animal patterns for each child and cut out.

Directions:
1. Discuss the concept of marsupials with the children. Read to them from a book about Australian animals.
2. Have the children each choose an animal to draw. They can look at pictures in a book or the animal patterns for ideas.
3. Give each child a small envelope to glue or tape to the center of their animal. This is their marsupial's pouch. Children can choose a cut-out baby animal pattern from the patterns provided to color and keep in their marsupial's pocket.
4. Post the completed animal pictures on an "Awesome Australia" bulletin board. Set out any available stuffed or plastic Australian animal toys near the display.

Option:
The eucalyptus is an aromatic tree that comes from Australia; eucalyptus-scented candles are often available at health food stores or garden centers. If available, you might burn a candle for the children, so that they can smell the interesting scent.

Book Link:
• *Wonderful Animals of Australia* illustrated by John Sibbick (National Geographic Society, 1990).
This pop-up book is filled with interesting information.
• *Koala* by Caroline Arnold, photos by Richard Hewett (William Morrow, 1987). Children will fall in love with the adorable koalas in this book.

AUSTRALIAN ANIMAL PATTERNS

CHILDREN IN CHINA

Teacher's Note:
Discuss the fact that in China people often live with their extended families. They see their grandparents, aunts, uncles, and cousins daily! School is held every day of the week, except Sunday. After school, children often go to recreation areas called Children's Palaces.

Materials:
Poster board, crayons, scissors, glue, sugar cubes, glitter

Preparation:
Cut a 6" poster board square for each child.

Directions:
1. Have the children plan their own version of a Children's Palace. Your little architects can design their ideal buildings for fun and recreation.
2. Children can glue the sugar cubes together to form the palace.
3. Silver or multicolored glitter can add beauty to the buildings.
4. When the palaces are finished, have the children sit with them on the rug. Ask, "What kinds of games can you play inside this palace?"

Option:
Celebrate the Chinese New Year! Give each child a copy of the dragon pattern, crayons or markers, glitter, and glue. Let the children decorate the dragon to create their own unique look. Post the completed dragon pictures on a "Gung Hay Fat Choy!" (Happy New Year!) bulletin board.

Book Link:
• *Chinese New Year* by Tricia Brown, photographs by Fran Ortiz (Holt, 1987). The Chinese New Year, which falls between mid-January and mid-February, is a time of celebration, and "Gung hay fat choy!" is the way to say "Good fortune and happiness!"
• *Gung Hay Fat Choy* by June Behrens (Children's Press, 1982).
Fierce dragons lead the Chinese New Year parade in this book of color photographs and short text.

DRAGON PATTERN

CHILDREN'S ZOO IN ISRAEL

Teacher's Note:
Describe life on an Israeli kibbutz, a family-like community where people live and work together. Everyone on the kibbutz has a specific job, including children. The children look after the animals in the farm and their pets in the children's zoo: rabbits, monkeys, geese, ducks, and donkeys.

Materials:
Israeli zoo patterns, green poster board, tagboard or stiff paper, tape, scissors, markers, crayons

Preparation:
Duplicate the pattern page onto tagboard or stiff paper (one per child).

Directions:
1. Let each child color and cut out a copy of the Israeli zoo patterns.
2. Provide green poster board squares for children to decorate with markers to create the animals' homes.
3. Children can tape their animals to the green poster board.
4. Display the Children's Zoos on a low table with the title "Israel Is Inviting!"

Option:
Children's Zoos can also be made in shoe boxes.

Book Link:
• *A Kibbutz in Israel* by Allegra Taylor, photographs by Nancy Durrell McKenna (Lerner, 1987).
This book is filled with pictures and information about a kibbutz.

• *Zoo Babies* text and photographs by Donna K. Grosvenor (National Geographic, 1978).
This adorable book for "young explorers" takes children on a photographic visit to a zoo.

ISRAELI ZOO PATTERNS

GOOD LUCK IN JAPAN

Teacher's Note:
Take children on an imaginary trip to Japan. Many Japanese houses have a place for good luck, decorated with ferns, oranges, and folded strips of paper. Ask if children have their own "lucky spots" at home.

Materials:
One small cardboard box for each child, orange and green construction paper, scissors, curling ribbon, star stickers, glue, foil, tempera paints, paintbrushes, glitter

Preparation:
Cut orange-sized orange construction paper circles. Cut simple leaf shapes from the green construction paper. Curl strands of ribbon.

Directions:
1. Give the children cardboard boxes to decorate as their own personal "lucky spots." They can begin by painting their boxes.
2. After the paint dries, children can glue on the orange construction paper circles, green leaves, and curling ribbons.
3. Glitter, aluminum foil, and sticky stars can further enhance their "lucky spots."
4. Display the completed boxes on a table with a "Lucky! Lucky!" label.

Option:
Ask children to bring in their own personal lucky charms, ornaments, coins, rabbit's feet, etc. They can share their lucky items before storing them in their lucky boxes.

HOLA = HELLO IN MEXICO

Teacher's Note:
Describe a day (*una dia*) in Mexico. Tortillas are often eaten with each meal. People take a *siesta* between two and four, when shops close, streets empty, and people rest. Handshakes are very important in Mexico. Have the children gently shake a friend's hand and say, "*Hola, amigo!*" to a boy or "*Hola, amiga!*" to a girl.

Materials:
Tortillas (flour and corn), chopped tomatoes, mild salsa, grated cheese, chopped olives, avocados, shredded lettuce, paper plates, serving spoons and forks

Preparation:
Place the above items on a low table.

Directions:
1. Invite children to a tortilla party. Ask each child to bring in a different filling, such as those mentioned above.
2. Cut flour and corn tortillas in half and heat them in an oven or microwave.
3. Let children sample the different kinds of tortillas and toppings. (Melt the cheese on the tortillas for children who want it.)
4. After children are finished eating, sing "Hola, Amigo" (amiga canta) to the tune of "This Is the Way We Wash Our Hands."

Hola, Amigo
Hola, amigo, como esta?
Como esta? como esta?
Hola, amigo, como esta?
Muy bien, gracias!

Book Link:
• *Let's Go: A Book in Two Languages— Vamos Un Libro en Dos Lenguas* by Rebecca Emberley (Little, 1993).
This informative, colorful book is told in English and Spanish.

HOUSES IN GHANA

Teacher's Note:

Describe the style of architecture in Ghana, Africa. There are brown mud houses surrounded by palm forests. In some homes, everyday items are decorated with designs and color, even chairs and combs and the most basic utensils. The houses themselves are often painted in colorful patterns.

Materials:

African house pattern, round boxes (oatmeal or coffee canisters work well), paper coffee filters, glue, butcher paper, scissors, black felt pen, paint or watercolors, paintbrushes

Preparation:

None.

Directions:

1. Show the children pictures of African houses from *Ashanti to Zulu*.
2. Children can create their own African home from a round container with a coffee filter lid. Provide watercolors or tempera paints and paintbrushes for the children to paint them. Encourage the use of many colors! The roofs should be painted yellow or straw colors to look thatched. (Note: If there aren't enough round containers available, children can color in the African house pattern.)
3. When the houses are dry, have the children sit together on the rug. In turn, each child can hold up his or her home and describe what might be going on inside.

Book Link:

• *Ashanti to Zulu* by Margaret Musgrove (Dial, 1976).
This Caldecott-medal book explains some traditions and customs of 26 African tribes from A to Z.

AFRICAN HOUSE PATTERN

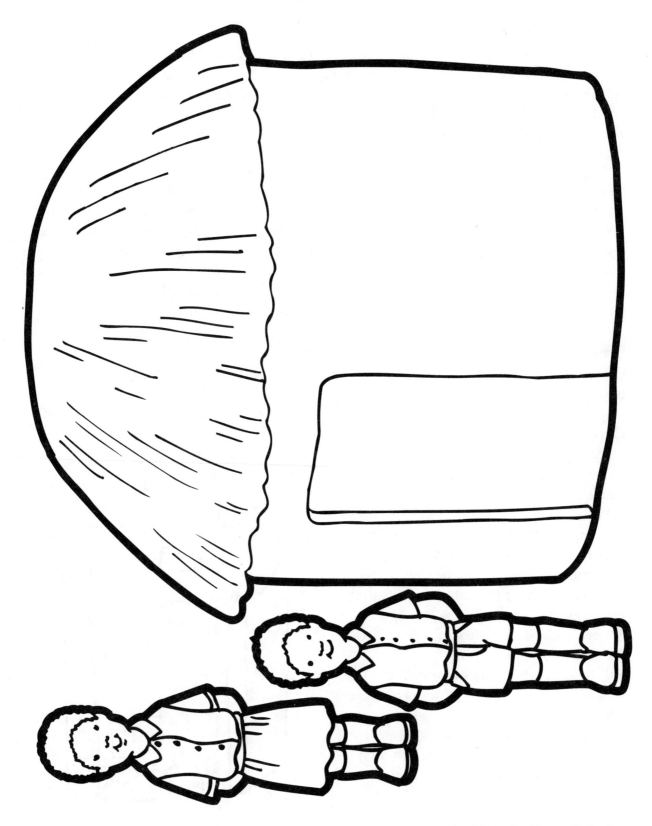

LIFE IN THE RAIN FOREST

Teacher's Note:

Describe a communal house in the Amazon forest, built from tree bark and palm leaves. Many families might live in the same house, in the same way that many animals might share the same tree "house" as they do in *The Great Kapok Tree*, below. Forest-dwelling children play outside and learn to garden, to hunt for wild honey, and to travel through the forest. They are given secret names, sometimes the names of animals or flowers.

Materials:

Amazon animal patterns, large empty box (such as a refrigerator box), tempera paint (green and brown), paintbrushes, construction paper squares (green and brown), scissors, crayons, Popsicle sticks, glue, tape, leaves, twigs, weeds, rocks

Preparation:

Enlarge and duplicate the pattern page for each child.

Directions:

1. Have the children work together to paint the box to look like a tree—brown trunk and green on top.
2. When the tree has dried, provide brown and green construction paper squares for children to tape like pockets (three sides with the open side facing up) to the tree. Children can glue the nature objects to the tree as well.
3. Give each child a sheet of animal patterns to color and cut out.
4. Provide Popsicle sticks for children to glue to the back of their patterns to make simple puppets.
5. Have the children put their puppets in the pockets on the tree. (Make sure that they put the puppets in appropriate

"level" pockets: the animals that live in the canopy should be near the top of the box, while the animals that live in trunks should be in the brown portion.)
6. Read *The Great Kapok Tree*. Children can take turns removing their puppets and speaking in the voices of the animals.

Book Link:

• *The Great Kapok Tree* by Lynne Cherry (Harcourt, 1990).
This rain forest tale is told by the animals of the Amazon.

AMAZON ANIMAL PATTERNS

canopy

canopy

forest floor

canopy

understory

canopy

understory

PERFUME IN FRANCE

Teacher's Note:
Tell the children that the French are especially proud of their perfume. Ask children to think about smells that they like. They can list all of the different kinds of scents they can think of, from the smell of their grandma's cookies to the way their baby sister or brother smells after a bath.

Note:
This activity should be set up at the water table. Let children work together to create a new fragrance. If possible, provide small containers with lids for children to use to take home their "signature scents."

Materials:
Plastic jugs, plastic tub or water table, measuring cups and spoons, sieves, eyedroppers, food coloring, scented waters such as rose water and Lily of the Valley (or extracts: lemon, vanilla, almond, etc.), water

Directions:
1. Set the measuring cups, spoons, eyedroppers, and sieves at the water table.
2. Fill small plastic jugs with water and add a few drops of food coloring to each one to make a range of colors.
3. Add a few drops of rose water to one bottle, Lily of the Valley to another, and so on. Place these jugs at the water table station.
4. Let children take turns mixing the colored, scented water in a tub or at the water table. (Note: Change the clear water at the table often, so that new children will have a clean starting place.)

5. If possible, bring in examples of real flowers for children to smell. Rank children's favorite flowers on a simple graph.

Book Link:
• *The Flower Alphabet Book* by Jerry Pallotta, illustrated by Leslie Evans (Charlesbridge, 1988).
This ABC book is filled with informative pictures about flowers.

SPICES FROM INDIA

Teacher's Note:
Describe the types of food that are eaten in India. Meals are often vegetarian, and cooks use spices such as curry, cinnamon, cumin, and ginger. Cows are considered sacred and wander throughout the city. Have children imagine what might happen if cows wandered freely in our cities!

Materials:
Rice, curry, cinnamon, cumin, ginger, raisins, nuts, forks, paper plates or bowls

Preparation:
Make enough rice for each child to have a serving.

Directions:
1. Place the spices, dried fruit, and nuts on a low table.
2. Serve a helping of rice to each child.
3. Encourage the children to try the different seasonings and toppings on their rice.
4. Ask the children, "What spice do you like the best?" "Is there a flavor you don't like?" Explain that people from different families can develop different tastes.

Book Link:
• *India Celebrates!* by Jane Werner Watson, illustrated by Susan Andersen (Garrard, 1974).
This resource book is filled with information about celebrations in India.
• *Take a Trip to India* by Keith Lye (Franklin Watts, 1982).
This is an informative India resource.

OUR WORLD CLASS PROJECT

Teacher's Note:
This final project uses the results of many of the activities from the "Children from Many Lands" chapter. Allow children to do as much of the work as possible in assembling this "classroom world." Invite parents, friends, and other classes to admire the completed work.

Materials:
Completed projects from this unit, patterns of children from other countries (found on the pattern pages in this chapter), crayons or markers, globe, construction paper, posting tools (tape, yarn, etc.), paper, pen

Preparation:
Clear low tables and a bulletin board for the display. Duplicate the multicultural children patterns.

Directions:
1. Help the children organize their work from this unit. They can set up their Amazon, Australian, Chinese, Ghanian, and Israeli structures on low tables. Provide colored construction paper for the background.
2. Construct a multicultural bulletin board for a backdrop. Children can color the children patterns and post them on the board.
3. Display the Japanese "Lucky Spots" on another table.
4. Set a globe or world map nearby so that observers can find the different countries represented.

5. Children can compose a brief description of their artwork display, each listing feelings about the completed work. Copy their statements onto a program and duplicate for classroom guests.

Option:
Sing a round of "It's a Small World!"

CHAPTER FOUR: FUN AND GAMES AROUND THE WORLD

All over the world, children play games with each other. Some games use equipment, such as jump ropes, jacks, and balls. Others require specific playing grounds or boundaries, such as Hopscotch, tennis, or baseball. Still other games require nothing but the presence of children, and these are some of the best-loved games of all: Tag; Duck, Duck, Goose; Hide and Seek; and so on.

Activities in this chapter introduce children to games of other countries and cultures. Children will develop a sense of global travel and geography through these creative and interactive experiences. And, best of all, they will have FUN!

DELIVER THE LETTER

Teacher's Note:
Discuss and list the information found on envelopes: name, street address, city, state, Zip code, country. Underline "country." Point out the fact that a country is bigger than its states or towns. To help children grasp this concept, draw a map of North America on the chalkboard and point out their country, state, city, and neighborhood.

Materials:
Envelopes (one per child), pencils, drawing paper, crayons

Preparation:
None.

Directions:
1. Give the children each an envelope and help them write their address on it. (They might want to practice first copying a sample that you write on scratch paper.) Note: Aides can assist children who aren't writing yet.
2. Have children trade envelopes with friends.
3. Provide drawing paper and crayons for children to use to draw pictures for their friends.
4. Show children how to fold their pictures and insert them in the envelopes as gifts for their friends.
5. Collect all the envelopes and "deliver the mail," giving each child the self-addressed envelope with the surprise inside.

Option 1:
Collect canceled stamps for children to glue or tape to their envelopes. Children can also make stamps from colored paper.

Option 2:
Take a field trip to a post office to see "behind the scenes" in the day of a mail carrier, or invite a mail carrier to talk with the children. Or walk to a blue mailbox and mail a letter to the class. Wait for it to arrive!

Book Link:
• *The Jolly Postman: Or Other People's Letters* by Janet and Allan Ahlberg (Little, Brown, 1986).
A jolly postman delivers letters to famous fairy tale characters.

FLAG FLYING

Teacher's Note:
Describe a piece of cloth that has a special color and design. Ask children to guess what it is: a flag. Explain that countries have their own flags, and that flags stand as their country's symbol. People are proud of their country's flag.

Materials:
Flag patterns, white paper, crayons or markers, tape

Preparation:
Duplicate the flag patterns for each child.

Directions:
1. Give each child a page of flag patterns to color. Children can color the flags in the colors they choose, or they can look in books to see the real colors of each flag.
2. Let children design their own personal flags on white sheets of paper.
3. When the children are finished, have them sit together on the rug. Each child, in turn, can show his or her personal flag and explain what it stands for.
4. Tape the colored flags, side by side, on a wall. Have the children observe the many different flags, the ones from real countries and the flags of their own invention!

Option:
Discuss the nicknames we have for the American flag: "Old Glory" and "Stars and Stripes," and the songs that have been written about it: "You're a Grand Old Flag," "Stars and Stripes Forever," "Oh, Say Can You See?"

FLAG PATTERNS

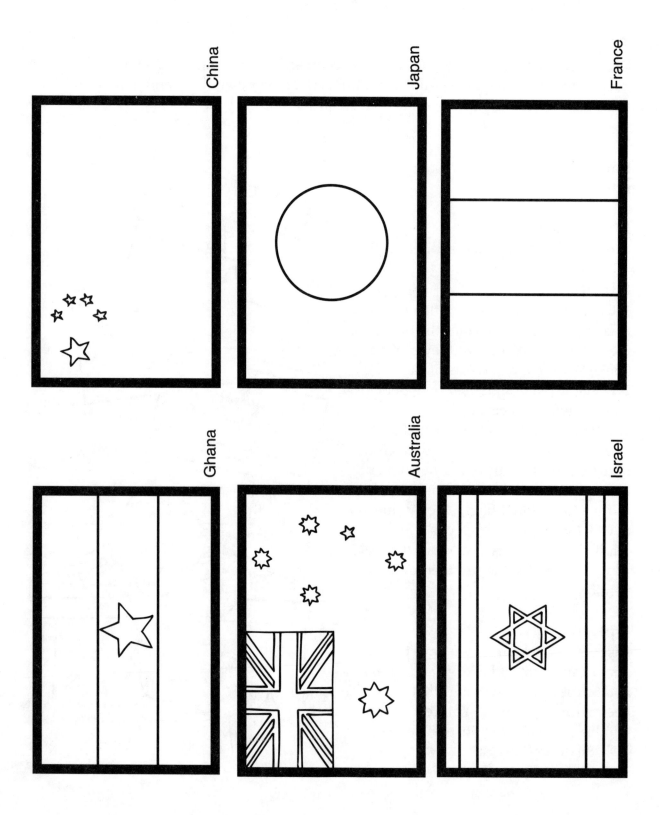

China

Japan

France

Ghana

Australia

Israel

JOHNNY IN THE INK POT

Teacher's Note:
Talk about games people play without props, such as, "Simple Simon" and "Duck, Duck, Goose." Many such games are invented in different countries. Some games are so much fun and so popular that they're played all over the world! "Johnny in the Ink Pot" is a game that's played in England.

Materials & Preparation:
None.

Directions:
1. Have the children sit together in a circle. Choose one child to stand away from the group so he or she can't see or hear group members.
2. Have the other children think of something to do using body movements, such as, washing dishes, painting a picture, or bouncing a ball. (This part is a bit like Charades.)
3. The group of children then says the following chant: "Johnny in the ink pot, what shall we do today?" (They should substitute the name of the hiding child for "Johnny.")
4. "Johnny" comes forward and says, "Get to work!"
5. The children in the circle now pretend to do whichever action was chosen, washing dishes, for example.
6. "Johnny" tries to guess what the children are doing.
7. If "Johnny" guesses incorrectly, the children can give clues until "Johnny" guesses the answer.
8. "Johnny" then picks another child to wait in the "ink pot."

Option:
Have the children base their action on a subject you are learning in the classroom. For example, if you are learning about animals, the children can make only animal gestures. If you are learning about transportation, they can pretend to be driving cars or buses, riding bicycles, and so on.

LOOKING GOOD

Teacher's Note:
Show pictures from fashion magazines to the class. Point out hair styles, clothing, jewelry, makeup, etc. Explain that people have different ways and reasons to decorate themselves. For example, some people from Sudan paint their bodies and faces to feel strong. What looks good to us might look funny to someone from another country! Discuss the idea that different cultures find beauty in different things.

Materials:
Face paints, mirrors, smocks, dress-up clothes (dresses, robes, fancy hats, shoes), recorded music

Preparation:
None.

Directions:
1. Let children dress up in clothes that make them feel beautiful.
2. Have children put on smocks and then help them paint their faces. (They can observe their transformation in a mirror.)
3. When each child has a painted face, have the children hold a mini-fashion show. Children can take turns sitting in the audience and parading to music.

Option:
Make decorative necklaces to wear. Give everyone a handful of colorful paper clips. Have them connect the paper clips together to form a chain. As an alternative, children can form shorter chain bracelets. Children can also string beads, macaroni, or Cheerios.

PLAYING YOTÉ

Teacher's Note:
Have the children, in turn, share their favorite game. Ask each child to tell you whether it is an indoor or outdoor game, how many people can play, and why the game is fun. Point out that children who live in different countries play games also.

Materials:
Sandbox, 12 pebbles, 12 small sticks

Preparation:
Scoop out five rows of six holes each in a sand box. The holes should be at least two inches deep.

Directions:
1. Explain that Yoté is a game played in Africa.
2. Choose two players. Give one player the 12 pebbles. Give the other player the 12 sticks.
3. The player with the pebbles starts the game by placing a pebble in any one of the holes.
4. The other player places a stick in any one of the holes.
5. The pebble player can now move his or her pebble or place another pebble in a hole. The object is to capture an opponent's piece by jumping over it. (This is similar to Chinese Checkers.)
6. Players continue to move their pieces that are already in the game, or take a turn by adding another of their playing pieces.
7. Players can make their pieces jump up or down, left or right, or diagonally. The game ends when a player has captured all the opponent's playing pieces.

8. As an option, the children can divide into two teams. Each team, in turn, can place a counter in a hole.

Option:
To make this an indoor game, draw the 30 circles on a sheet of poster board. Use pebbles and sticks or pennies with different colored sticky stars for markers.

THERE WAS AN OLD LADY

Teacher's Note:
Ask the children if they have eaten any food today. Explain that if they travelled to another country, they would eat different kinds of foods. Ask the children to tell you the strangest thing they've ever eaten and liked, for example, scrambled eggs and jelly. Describe some delicacies in other countries, including monkey brains, spiders, tripe, and so on.

Materials & Preparation:
None.

Directions:
1. Teach children to sing this new version of "I Know an Old Lady. . ."
2. Have children help you think up new versions to the song.

There Was an Old Lady
There was an old lady who swallowed
   a fly,
She thought it was tasty and went on
   to try
A great heaping plate of spiders,
   deep-fried.
"I think they're terrific," that old lady
   cried!

She ordered a platter of grasshopper
   stew,
And liked it a lot, but then, wouldn't
   you?

Option 1:
Have a tasting party with food popular in different countries. Offer rice from China, noodles from Italy, sausage or pumpernickel bread from Germany, goat milk from Sweden, Swiss cheese, sushi from Japan, and so on.

Option 2:
Have children discuss the types of foods they like and try to figure out the origins, for example, ask if children really think that French fries are from France.

TO MARKET, TO MARKET

Teacher's Note:
Discuss the concept of money. Explain that in different countries, money has different names. Teach the children the following names for money: "rupee" (India), "drachma" (Greece), "lira" (Italy), "peso" (Spain), "schilling" (Austria), "rouble" (Russia), "shekel" (Israel), "yen" (Japan).

Materials:
Money patterns, shoe box, different colored paper, scissors, "sale" items (small toys, a scarf, a jump rope, blocks, books, and so on)

Preparation:
Place the "sale" items on a low table. Place the shoe box nearby for the cash register. Duplicate the money patterns onto different colors of paper, laminate, and cut out.

Directions:
1. Explain to the children that the table is a store, and that the items are not to keep.
2. Give each child a few pieces of paper money.
3. Let children pretend that the store is in another country. Give them money in a different color and have them call it by one of the terms they've learned, "shekels," for example.
4. Continue to change money colors and money words until every child has had the chance to "buy" items.

Option 1:
Discuss the concept of bartering and give children a chance to trade items amongst themselves.

Option 2:
Bring in coins from different countries (or ask children to). Let the children observe the coins and make rubbings of them.

©1995 Monday Morning Books, Inc.

MONEY PATTERNS

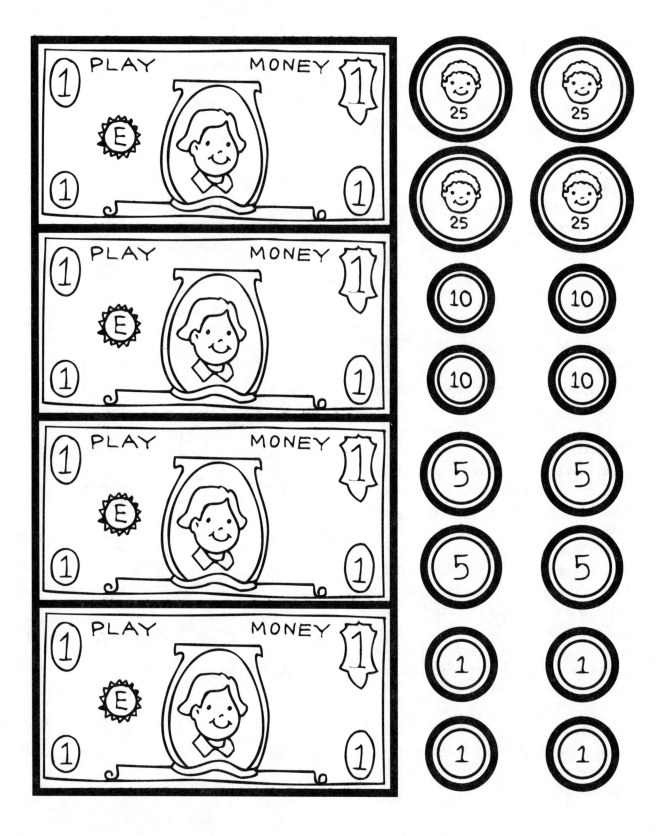

TRAVELING 'ROUND AND 'ROUND

Teacher's Note:
Discuss the different transportation options that people choose from when traveling between countries. Examples: trains, planes, cars, boats, hovercrafts, etc. Have children list the kinds of transportation they have used themselves. Ask them to name the type they'd most like to try in the future.

Materials:
Globe

Preparation:
None.

Directions:
1. Have the children sit together on the rug.
2. Teach them to sing "The Traveling Song," to the tune of "Here We Go Loopty Loo." As you sing, twirl the globe around and around. Have the children pretend to be circling the world in small airplanes. They can stretch their arms out and tilt back and forth as they walk around.

The Traveling Song
Traveling 'round and 'round,
Traveling 'round and 'round,
Traveling 'round and 'round,
And landing on the ground!

3. Choose a child traveler to stop the globe by putting a finger on it. Tell the children that the planes they are traveling in have just landed.
4. Say the name of the country that was picked. If possible, look up facts about the country in an encyclopedia and share the information with the children. If a child stops the globe in an ocean, read to the

children about that ocean. The children can then pretend that they are traveling by boat.
5. Spin the globe again and let another child traveler stop the globe.
6. Continue until each child has had a chance to chose a destination.

WHAT WE WEAR

Teacher's Note:
Ask the children if they think the weather affects what they decide to wear. Explain that clothes are often worn to suit a particular climate, for example, if the climate is very cold, people wear layers of thick clothes, boots, high collars, and ear flaps!

Materials:
People paper doll patterns, clothes patterns, heavy and lightweight paper, crayons or markers, scissors

Preparation:
Duplicate the people patterns onto heavy paper for each child. Duplicate a set of the clothes patterns onto lightweight paper for each child.

Directions:
1. Let the children decorate all the patterns with crayons or markers.
2. Help children cut out their paper people and clothing.
3. Children can mix and match the clothing with the dolls, deciding what type of clothing is required for a specific kind of weather. Start this activity by announcing that it is hot, cool, or rainy and letting the children choose the appropriate attire for their dolls.

Option:
Provide different kinds of clothes in the dramatic play corner for children to use.

Book Link:
• *Animals Should Definitely Not Wear Clothing* by Judi and Ron Barrett (Atheneum, 1970).
This silly book shows many reasons why animals should remain bare!

PEOPLE PATTERNS

CLOTHES PATTERNS

YOUR PASSPORT, PLEASE
CLASS PROJECT

Teacher's Note:
Have the children brainstorm the different ways that people identify themselves. For example, people have first and last names, drivers' licenses, and passports. Discuss the fact that people need passports to travel between countries because passports show who they are.

Materials:
Passport patterns, dark blue paper, glue, crayons, markers, rubber stamps, colored ink pads (option: Polaroid or school photographs of the children)

Preparation:
Duplicate the passport patterns onto dark blue paper so that each child has one.

Directions:
1. Give each child a copy of the passport pattern.
2. Show the children how to fold the pattern in half so that the place for their picture is on the inside.
3. Children can decorate the plain outside of the passport with crayons or markers.
4. In the box inside, children can draw their self-portrait. Or let children glue their school photo or a cut-out Polaroid inside the square.
5. Set up different areas of the classroom for children to "travel" to as they pretend to travel between countries. The book corner could be one country, the block corner another, and so on. You can differentiate these areas with flags (pp. 67-68) from the countries. Children can take turns being travelers and customs officials. The customs officials can stamp the travelers' passports with rubber stamps.

6. Children can collect different colored stamps in their passports.

Option 1:
If possible, let children observe a real passport.

Option 2:
Duplicate copies of the passport pattern and let children make additional passports for classroom animals, pets, friends, etc.

PASSPORT PATTERNS

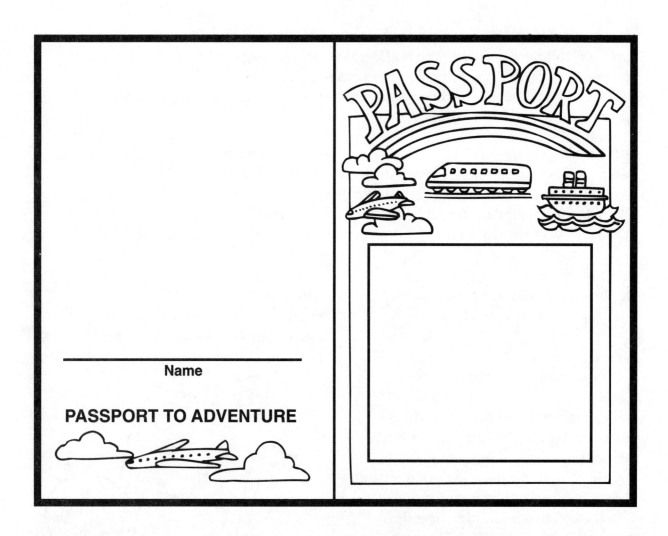

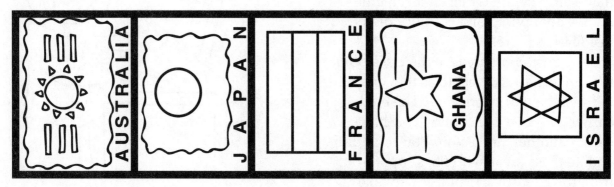

©1995 Monday Morning Books, Inc.